Contents

Recordings of all No Notes music can be heard at www.NoNotes.uk

Why No Notes?

The piano is a fantastically rewarding instrument to play. It's also a challenge. There are so many notes to choose from and so many fingers to co-ordinate! **No Notes** piano music is designed to help absolute beginners of all ages make a good start learning a variety of challenging foundation keyboard skills (see page opposite).

No Notes piano music is a kind of tablature or 'tab'. Each piece includes a 'keyboard map' showing where to put your hands and a 'song chart' showing which fingers and thumbs to use and when (see page 5). Beginners like tab because unlike standard staff-notated piano music with its clefs, lines and spaces, time signatures, key signatures, notes, rests and such, **No Notes** tab shows beginners simply which piano keys to push and when. It also makes *interesting* musical and technical challenges more accessible to absolute beginners than staff notation can.

Reading music is one among *several* foundation keyboard skills and beginners can quickly become frustrated, overwhelmed and deterred if all these new challenging skills are presented through the (opaque) prism of staff-notated piano music. In fact, if beginners are asked to use standard piano music too soon it is often, ironically, their musical literacy that suffers

most! Bamboozled by unfamiliar symbols and so many lines and spaces, beginners often end up playing by ear rather than by reading the music on the page. And once a student begins to ignore notation and to learn pieces by ear routinely it can become harder and harder for them to achieve a useful level of musical literacy as the pieces they play become more and more complex.

Easy-reader books provide simple engaging narratives which help children understand how written words and spoken words relate to each other. In a similar way, easy-to-read **No Notes** piano music helps absolute beginners understand how reading music enables them to play familiar song melodies and cool, bluesy riffs and grooves.

No Notes beginners learn quickly not only how to use all their fingers and thumbs to make music but also that written music is an enabling support rather than a tiresome and difficult obstacle. And because **No Notes** piano music incorporates several important features of staff-notated piano music, **No Notes** graduates are both motivated and prepared to make the transition from **No Notes** to standard piano music in due course. Learning valuable foundation keyboard skills has never been so simple and so much fun!

Foundation keyboard skills

Navigating the piano keyboard - Beginners need to make sense of the bewildering array of black and white keys on a piano keyboard. Each **No Notes** piano piece includes a 'keyboard map' showing players where their fingers and thumbs go. These maps, which vary from piece to piece, provide lots of opportunities for beginners to practise moving around the keyboard placing their hands over the correct keys.

Learning to read music - Beginners need to learn that reading music can be as fun and rewarding as reading words. **No Notes** piano music is very easy to understand and so helps beginners build confidence in their ability to make musical sense of written music. And because **No Notes** piano music incorporates several important features of staff-notated piano music, **No Notes** graduates are both motivated and prepared to make the transition from **No Notes** to standard piano music in due course.

Playing without looking at fingers and thumbs - Beginners need to learn to 'find their fingers' without looking - they will be playing more than one note at a time soon! **No Notes** piano music helps beginners do this - either hands do not move once placed (*No Notes* song books), or else the same sequence of digits plays in different hand positions (*No Notes Blues Primer*).

Playing in time - Beginners need to learn how to play in time, accurately and precisely. **No Notes** piano music supports rhythmical playing in three ways: by showing all *beats* as equally-spaced vertical lines; by showing the *count* for each piece ('in' 2, 3 or 4) as thicker regularly-spaced vertical lines; by showing longer and shorter duration sounds as variations in the horizontal distance between finger numbers.

Developing even-handedness - Pianists use the fingers and thumbs of both hands and beginners need to learn how to 'lead' with any of their ten digits. All **No Notes** piano music gives equal importance to the fingers and thumbs of both hands.

Learning to practise - Beginners need to learn how to tackle musical challenges and develop good practising habits. **No Notes**' simplicity helps beginners understand how to make things right when they go wrong.

Playing musically - Musicians do not simply push the correct notes at the correct time. Wonder and delight come from 'finding your voice'. **No Notes**' combination of attractive, familiar music and simple notation helps beginners learn to play with the same control and expression as when they sing, hum or whistle.

Getting started

Learn your finger numbers - Lay one hand, palm downwards, on a piece of paper and draw around your fingers and thumbs. Do the same for the other hand, then number the digits 1, 2, 3, 4 and 5, starting with '1' for each thumb. Hold both hands in front of you, palms downwards with digits extended, and ask a friend to touch different digits randomly. Practise to see how quickly you can say the correct number. Remember, your thumbs are both '1'. Repeat, with your eyes closed!

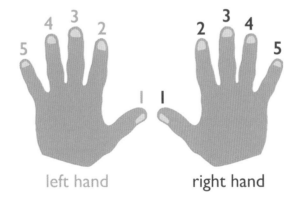

left hand   right hand

Know the tune - Choose a tune. If you are unsure how a song goes, listen to the recording available on **www.NoNotes.uk**. Try and sing the words as you are listening. This will help you to learn the melody. Once you know how a song goes you are ready to try and play it.

Make sure your hands are in the right place - The black keys on your keyboard are arranged in alternating groups of two and three. Each **No Notes** song includes a *keyboard map* showing where to place your hands. Always check this keyboard map - different songs may use different piano keys! Once they are in position your hands do not move.

keyboard map

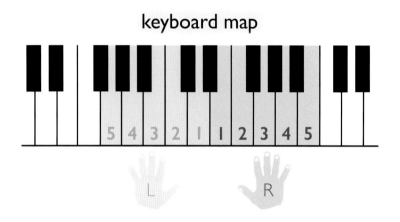

Reading the music - **No Notes** piano music uses *song charts* to show which fingers and thumbs to use and when. Piano keys for the Right hand, R , are written in Red <u>above</u> a line. Piano keys for the Left hand, L , are written in Lime green <u>below</u> the line. Read song charts from left to right and push keys under the digits indicated. A <u>wider gap</u> between two numbers means you <u>wait longer</u> before playing the second piano key.

song chart

R	1	2						1	2	
L	1		3	3	3	3	3	2	1	

Are you sitting comfortably?

Shoulders
Loose

Back
Upright and
relaxed

Elbows
At the same height
as the surface of
the white keys

Forearms
Parallel to
the floor

Seat
Without backrest or arms.
It should allow you to sit
comfortably at the correct
height for your Elbows

Feet
Flat on the floor or resting
securely on a flat support
(book/box/stool)

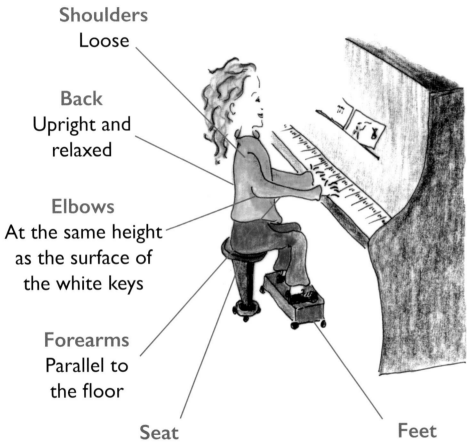

Wrists
Level with the back of your
hands and forearms (not bent
upwards or sagging down)

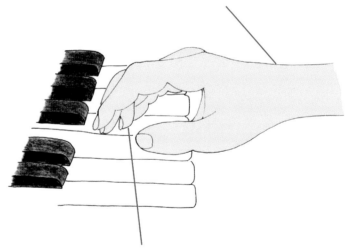

Fingers and thumbs
Imagine holding a large orange loosely
in your hand. Your fingers should be
curved and rest lightly on the keys. Push
keys with the sides of your thumbs

Getting the most out of No Notes

Develop good practising habits
- make the most of your time at the keyboard!

Sing songs before you play them. It makes them easier to play. Recordings of *No Notes* music can be heard at **www.NoNotes.uk**.

Clap a beat and sing finger and thumb numbers in time to the tune of the melody.

Play with one hand only. When the other hand has notes to play, tap your hand on your leg instead of pushing keys. Remember to swap hands over.

Say the number of the finger or thumb you are using out loud as you play.

Once you can play the first line of a piece, move on to the second line, the third line, and so on. Avoid playing over and over music you can play already.

Try not to look at your fingers and thumbs as you play. They *will* work without you watching!

Play No Notes duets

All **No Notes** music can be played as duets. One person plays one hand. Another person plays the other. It's half as hard and twice the fun!

Two players sit side-by-side at the piano. It is easier and more comfortable if the player sitting on the left (facing the piano) plays the *right* hand part and the player sitting on the right plays the *left* hand part (i.e. players' forearms cross over each other).

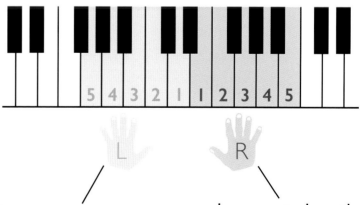

player seated on the *right* plays *left* hand part

player seated on the *left* plays *right* hand part

Allee-Allee-O

The big ship sails on **the Allee-Allee-O**,
The Allee-Allee-O, the Allee-Allee-O.
Oh, the big ship sails on the Allee-Allee-O
On the last day of September.

The captain said it will **never, never do, ...**

The big ship sank to **the bottom of the sea, ...**

A sailor
went to sea

A sailor went to sea, sea, sea
To see what he could see, see, see,
But all that he could see, see, see
Was the bottom of the deep blue sea, sea, sea.

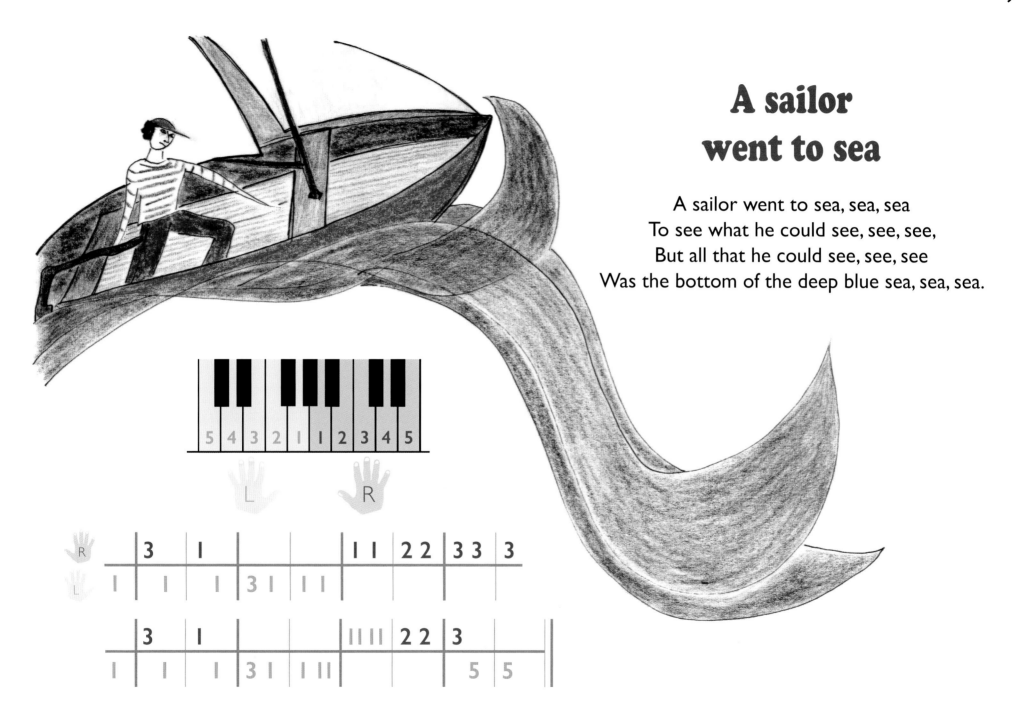

Baa baa black sheep

Baa baa black sheep
Have you any wool?
Yes Sir! Yes Sir!
Three bags full!

One for the Master
And one for the Dame.
One for the little boy
Who lives down the lane.

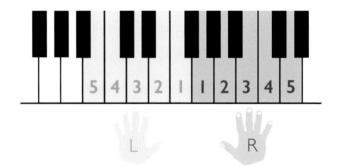

Bobbie Shafto

Bobbie Shafto's gone to sea,
Silver buckles on his knee.
He'll come back and marry me,
Bonnie Bobbie Shafto.
**Bobbie Shafto's bright and fair,
Combing down his yellow hair.
He's my love for evermore,
Bonnie Bobbie Shafto.**

Bobbie Shafto's tall and slim.
He's always dressed so neat and trim.
The lassies they all keek at him,
Bonnie Bobbie Shafto.
Bobbie Shafto's bright and fair, ...

Bobbie Shafto's gett'n a bairn,
For to dandle in his arm.
In his arm and on his knee,
Bobbie Shafto loves me.
Bobbie Shafto's bright and fair, ...

12

Frère Jacques

Frère Jacques, Frère Jacques,
Dormez-vous? Dormez-vous?
Sonnez les matines!
Sonnez les matines!
Din! Dan! Don! Din! Dan! Don!

_____

Are you sleeping? Are you sleeping?
Brother John, Brother John?
Morning bells are ringing!
Morning bells are ringing!
Ding! Dang! Dong! Ding! Dang! Dong!

_____

I hear thunder. I hear thunder.
Can you too? Can you too?
Pitter-patter raindrops!
Pitter-patter raindrops!
I'm wet through. So are you.

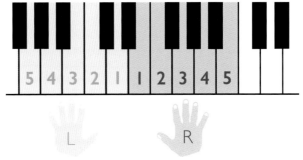

This song can be sung as a 4-part round. Each new voice begins when the voice immediately in front begins the second line.

R		1				1	
L 2	1		2	2	1		2
1	2	3		1	2	3	
3 4	3 2	1		3 4	3 2	1	
			2				2
2	5	2		2	5	2	

Girls and boys

Girls and boys come out to play.
The moon doth shine as bright as day.

Leave your supper and leave your sleep
And join your playfellows in the street.

Come with a whoop and come with a call.
Come with a good will or not at all.

Up the ladder and down the wall,
A halfpenny roll will serve us all.

You find milk and I'll find flour,
And we'll have a pudding in half an hour.

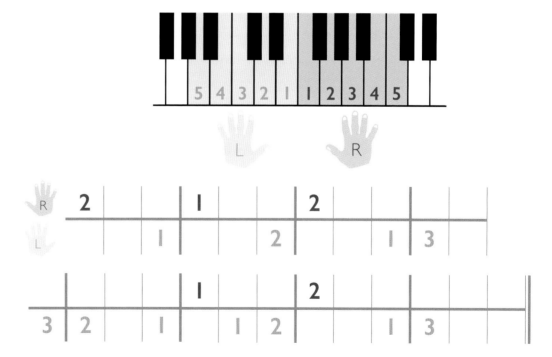

Goosey goosey gander

Goosey goosey gander,
Whither shall I wander?
Upstairs and downstairs
And in my lady's chamber.

There I met an old man
Who wouldn't say his prayers,
So I took him by his left leg
And threw him down the stairs.

Go tell Aunt Nancy

Go tell Aunt Nancy,
Go tell Aunt Nancy,
Go tell Aunt Nancy,
The old grey goose is dead.

The one she's been saving ...
To make a feather bed.

She died in the millpond ...
From standing on her head.

The goslings are crying ...
Because their mamma's dead.

The gander is weeping ...
Because his wife is dead.

Go tell Aunt Nancy ...
The old grey goose is dead.

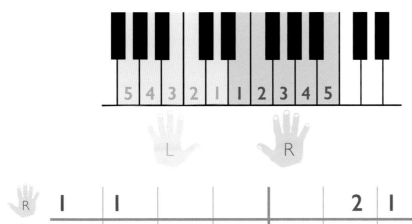

Here we go ...

Here we go round the mulberry bush,
The mulberry bush, the mulberry bush.
Here we go round the mulberry bush
On a cold and frosty morning.

———————

Here we go gathering nuts in May, ...

Who will you have for nuts in May, ...

We'll have [name] for nuts in May, ...

———————

This is the way we wash our hands, ...

This is the way we brush our teeth, ...

Hickory dickory dock!

Hickory dickory dock!
The mouse ran up the clock.
The clock struck one.
The mouse ran down.
Hickory dickory dock!

Hush, little baby

Hush, little baby, don't say a word!
Papa's gonna buy you a mockingbird.

And if that mockingbird won't sing,
Papa's gonna buy you a diamond ring.

And if that diamond ring turns brass,
Papa's gonna buy you a looking glass.

And if that looking glass gets broke,
Papa's gonna buy you a billy goat.

And if that billy goat won't pull,
Papa's gonna buy you a cart and bull.

And if that cart and bull turn over,
Papa's gonna buy you a dog named Rover.

And if that dog named Rover won't bark.
Papa's gonna buy you a horse and cart.

And if that horse and cart fall down,
You'll still be the sweetest little baby in town.

I love little pussy

I love little pussy.
Her coat is so warm
And if I don't hurt her
She'll do me no harm.

So I won't pull her tail
Nor scare her away,
But pussy and I
Very gently will play.

I'll sit by the fire
And give her some food,
And pussy will love me
Because I am good.

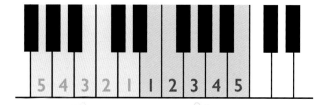

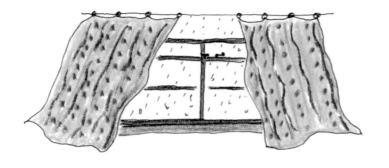

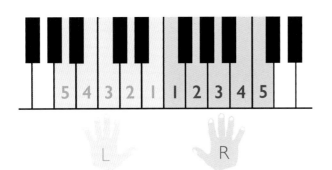

It's raining.
It's pouring

It's raining. It's pouring.
The old man is snoring.
He went to bed and bumped his head,
And couldn't get up in the morning.

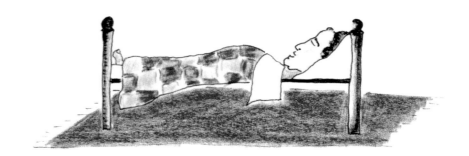

Jack and Jill

Jack and Jill went up the hill
To fetch a pail of water.
Jack fell down and broke his crown
And Jill came tumbling after.

Up Jack got and home did trot
As fast as he could caper;
Went to bed to mend his head
With vinegar and brown paper.

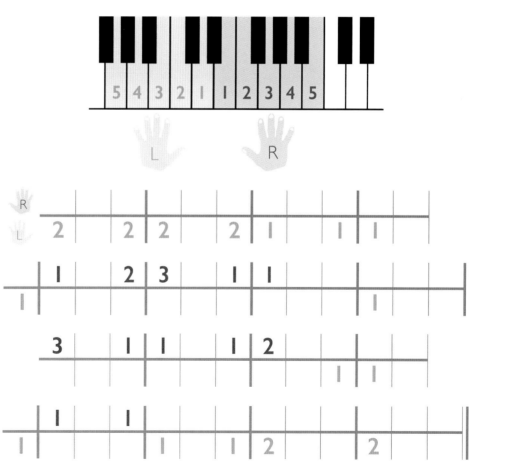

Lavender's blue

Lavender's blue, dilly dilly, lavender's green!
When I am king, dilly, dilly, you shall be queen.

Who told you so, dilly, dilly, who told you so?
'Twas my own heart, dilly, dilly, that told me so.

Call up your men, dilly, dilly, set them to work,
Some with a rake, dilly, dilly, some with a fork,

Some to make hay, dilly, dilly, some to thresh corn.
While you and I, dilly, dilly, keep ourselves warm.

Lavender's green, dilly, dilly, Lavender's blue!
If you love me, dilly, dilly, I will love you.

Let the birds sing, dilly, dilly, and the lambs play.
We shall be safe, dilly, dilly, out of harm's way.

I love to dance, dilly, dilly; I love to sing.
When I am queen, dilly, dilly, you'll be my king.

R	2	2	2	1		3	3	3	
L	3				1	23	3		

	2	2	2	1		1			
	3				1	23	1	2	3

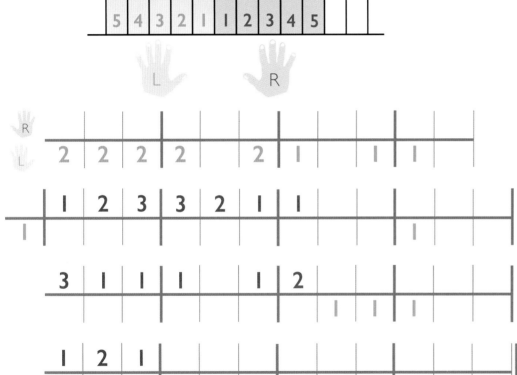

Little Bo-Peep

Little Bo-Peep
Has lost her sheep.
And doesn't know where to find them.
Leave them alone,
And they will come home,
Wagging their tails behind them.

Little Bo-Peep
Fell fast asleep
And dreamed she heard them bleating;
But when she awoke,
She found it a joke,
For they were still a-fleeting.

Then up she took
Her little crook,
Determined for to find them.
She found them indeed,
But it made her heart bleed,
For they'd left their tails behind them.

London Bridge is falling down

London Bridge is **falling down,**
Falling down, falling down.
London Bridge is falling down,
My fair lady.

Build it up with **wood and clay!** ...
Wood and clay will **wash away,** ...

Build it up with **bricks and mortar!** ...
Bricks and mortar **will not stay,** ...

Build it up with **iron and steel!** ...
Iron and steel will **bend and bow,** ...

Build it up with **silver and gold!** ...
Silver and gold will be **stolen away,** ...

Set a man to **watch all night!** ...
Suppose the man **should fall asleep,** ...
Give him a pipe to **smoke all night!** ...

London's burning!

London's burning! London's burning!
Fetch the engines! Fetch the engines!
    Fire! Fire! Fire! Fire!
Pour on water! Pour on water!

This song can be sung as a 4-part round. Each new voice begins when the voice immediately in front begins the second line.

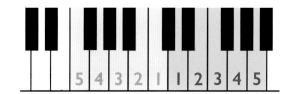

Mary had a **little lamb,**
Little lamb, little lamb.
Mary had a little lamb.
Its fleece was white as snow.

And everywhere that **Mary went, ...**
The lamb was sure to go.

It followed her to **school one day, ...**
Which was against the rules.

It made the children **laugh and play ...**
To see a lamb at school.

And so the teacher **turned it out, ...**
But still it lingered near.

And waited **patiently about ...**
'Til Mary did appear.

"Why does the lamb love **Mary so?"** ...
The eager children cry.

"Why, Mary loves the lamb, **you know."** ...
The teacher did reply.

Mary had a little lamb

Mary, Mary, quite contrary

4 4	2 2	3 3	1 1	2 22	4 2	1

			3	222	1 11	
4	3 2	1 4	3 2	1		1

Mary, Mary, quite contrary,
How does your garden grow?
With silver bells and cockle shells
And pretty maids all in a row.

My Bonnie lies over the ocean

My Bonnie lies over the ocean.
My Bonnie lies over the sea.
My Bonnie lies over the ocean.
O, bring back my Bonnie to me!
Bring back, bring back,
O, bring back my Bonnie to me, to me!
Bring back, bring back,
O, bring back my Bonnie to me!

O, blow the winds over the ocean
And blow the winds over the sea!
O, blow the winds over the ocean
And bring back my Bonnie to me!
Bring back, bring back ...

Last night as I lay on my pillow,
Last night as I lay on my bed,
Last night as I lay on my pillow,
I dreamt that my Bonnie was dead.
Bring back, bring back ...

The winds have blown over the ocean.
The winds have blown over the sea.
The winds have blown over the ocean
And brought back my Bonnie to me.
Bring back, bring back ...

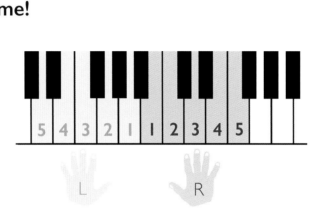

Oh dear, what can the matter be?

Oh dear, what can the matter be?
Dear, dear, what can the matter be?
Oh dear, what can the matter be?
Johnny's so long at the fair.

He promised he'd buy me a fairing should please me,
And then for a kiss, oh he vowed he would tease me.
He promised he'd bring me a bunch of blue ribbons
To tie up my bonny brown hair.
Oh dear, what can the matter be? ...

He promised he'd buy me a basket of posies,
A garland of lilies, a garland of roses;
A little straw hat to set off the blue ribbons
That tie up my bonny brown hair.
Oh dear, what can the matter be? ...

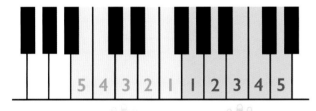

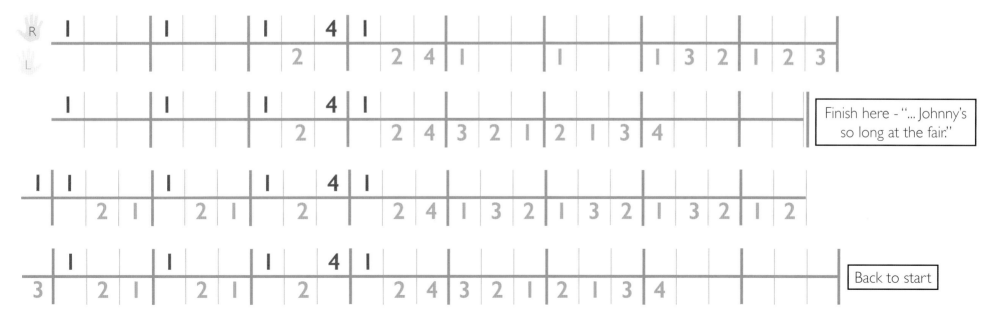

Finish here - "... Johnny's so long at the fair."

Back to start

Old MacDonald

Old MacDonald had a farm. Ee-i-ee-i-o!
And on that farm he had **a dog**. Ee-i-ee-i-o!
With a **woof** *woof* here and a *woof woof* there
Here a *woof*, there a *woof*, everywhere a *woof woof,*
Old MacDonald had a farm. Ee-i-ee-i-o!

... on that farm he had **some cows ...   ... moo**

... on that farm he had **a horse ...   ... neigh**

... on that farm he had **some sheep ...   ... baa**

... on that farm he had **some ducks ... ... quack**

... on that farm he had **a cat ...   ... miaow**

One, two, three, four, five

One, two, three, four, five,
Once I caught a fish alive.
Six, seven, eight, nine, ten,
Then I let it go again.

Why did you let it go?
Because it bit my finger so.
Which finger did it bite?
This little finger on my right.

Oranges and lemons

"Oranges and lemons"
Say the bells of St. Clement's.
"You owe me five farthings"
Say the bells of St. Martin's.

"When will you pay me?"
Say the bells of Old Bailey.
"When I grow rich"
Say the bells of Shoreditch.

"When will that be?"
Say the bells of Stepney.
"I do not know"
Says the Great Bell of Bow.

Polly, put the kettle on!

Polly, put the kettle on!
Polly, put the kettle on!
Polly, put the kettle on!
We'll all have tea.

Sukey, take it off again!
Sukey, take it off again!
Sukey, take it off again!
They've all gone away.

5 4 3 2 1 | 1 2 3 4 5
L   R

R: 4 5 | 4 3 2 | | 1 2 1 |
L: | 1 1 | | 1 2 4 4

R: 4 5 | 4 3 2 | 2 |
L: | 1 1 | 3 2 1

R: 2 | 3 1 2 | 3 1 |
L: 1 | 1 1 | 3 1 2 4 4

R: 2 | 3 1 2 | 2 |
L: 1 | 1 1 | 3 2 2 1

Ring-a-ring o' roses

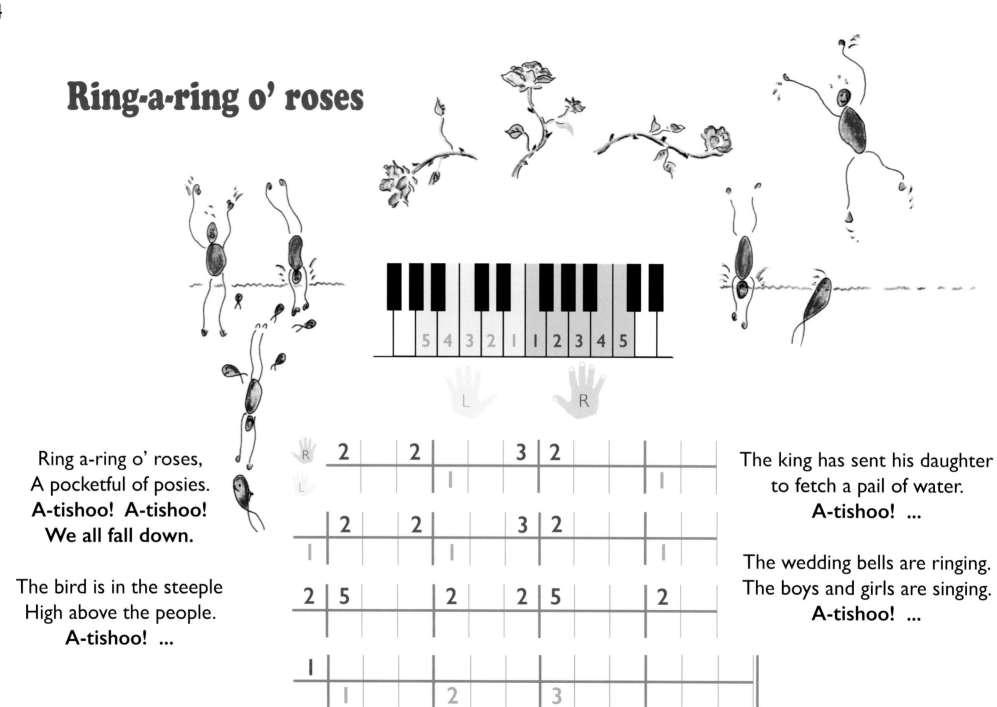

Ring a-ring o' roses,
A pocketful of posies.
A-tishoo! A-tishoo!
We all fall down.

The bird is in the steeple
High above the people.
A-tishoo! ...

The king has sent his daughter
to fetch a pail of water.
A-tishoo! ...

The wedding bells are ringing.
The boys and girls are singing.
A-tishoo! ...

Rock-a-bye baby

Rock-a-bye baby, on the treetops.
When the wind blows, the cradle will rock.
When the bough breaks, the cradle will fall
And down will come baby, cradle and all.

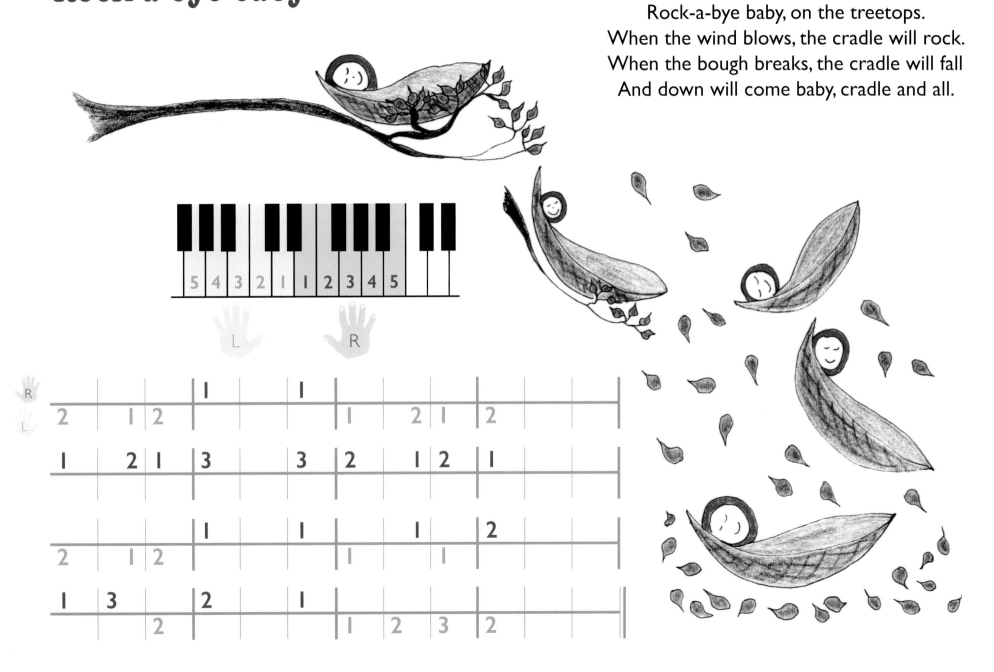

Row, row, row your boat

Row, row, row your boat
Gently down the stream.
Merrily! Merrily! Merrily! Merrily!
Life is but a dream.

Row, row, row your boat
Gently down the stream.
If you see a crocodile,
Don't forget to scream ...

... AARGHHH!

Skip to my Lou

Skip to my Lou, my chosen one!
Skip to my Lou, my chosen one!
Skip to my Lou, my chosen one!
Skip to my Lou, my darlin'!

Flies in the buttermilk; shoo, fly, shoo! ...

There's a little red wagon; paint it blue! ...

Cows in the cornfield; what'll I do? ...

Can't get a red bird; jay bird'll do ...

Cat's in the cream jar; Oo! Oo! Oo! ...

Lost my partner; what'll I do? ...

I'll get another one, prettier than you ...

Off to Texas, two by two! ...

Skip! Skip! Skip to my Lou! ...

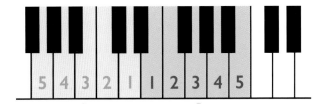

Ten green bottles

Ten green bottles
Standing on the wall.
Ten green bottles
Standing on the wall.
And if one green bottle
Should accidentally fall there'll be

Nine ...

Eight ...

Seven ...

Six ...

Five ...

Four ...

Three ...

Two ...

One ...

No green bottles
Standing on the wall.

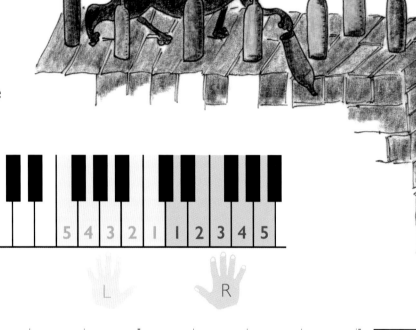

R				2		I		I	2	
L	I	I	I			I			I	

	2	2		2	4		3	2	3	4	2

	5	5		4	2		I	2	I		
I	I						I			I	3	4	3

FINISH HERE - "... no green bottles standing on the wall."

BACK TO START

The drunken sailor

What shall we do with the drunken sailor?
What shall we do with the drunken sailor?
What shall we do with the drunken sailor
Early in the morning?
Hoo-ray, and up she rises!
Hoo-ray, and up she rises!
Hoo-ray, and up she rises
Early in the morning!

Put him in the long boat
till he's sober! ... Hooray ...

Put him in the scuppers
with a hose-pipe on him! ... Hooray ...

Heave him by the leg
in a runnin' bowlin'! ... Hooray ...

Tie him to the taffrail
when she's yard-arm under! ... Hooray ...

Put him in the bilge
and make him drink it! ... Hooray ...

Soak 'im in oil
till he sprouts some flippers! ... Hooray ...

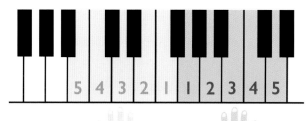

The farmer's in his dell

The farmer's in his dell.
The farmer's in his dell.
Ee-i-addee-o!
The farmer's in his dell.

The farmer wants a wife ...

The wife wants a child ...

The child wants a dog ...

The dog wants a bone ...

The grand old Duke of York

Oh, the grand old Duke of York,
He had ten thousand men.
He marched them up to the top of the hill,
And he marched them down again.

And when they were up, they were up.
And when they were down, they were down.
And when they were only half-way up,
They were neither up nor down.

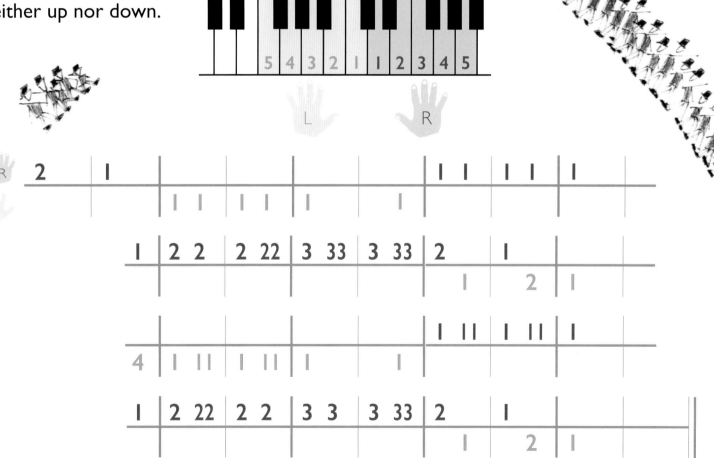

There's a hole in my bucket

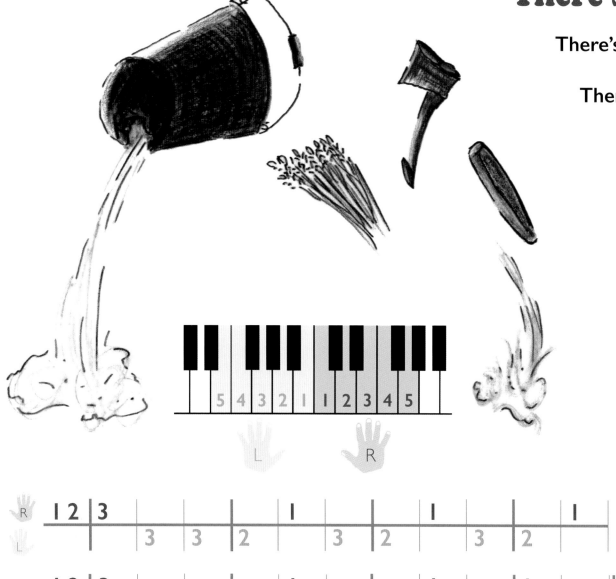

There's a hole in my bucket, dear Liza, *dear Liza.*
There's a hole in my bucket, dear Liza, a hole.
Then fix it, dear Henry, *dear Henry, dear Henry.*
Then fix it, dear Henry, dear Henry, fix it!

With what shall I fix it, dear Liza, ...?
With straw, dear Henry, ...

But the straw is too long, dear Liza, ...
Then cut it, dear Henry, ...

With what shall I cut it, dear Liza, ...?
With an axe, dear Henry, ...

But the axe is too dull, dear Liza, ...
Then hone it, dear Henry, ...

On what shall I sharpen it, dear Liza, ...?
On a stone, dear Henry, ...

But the stone is too dry, dear Liza, ...
Well wet it, dear Henry, ...

With what shall I wet it, dear Liza, ...?
With water, dear Henry, ...

In what shall I fetch it, dear Liza, ...?
In a bucket, dear Henry, ...

But there's a hole in my bucket, dear Liza, ...

The wheels on the bus

The **wheels** on the bus go **round and round,**
Round and round, round and round.
The wheels on the bus go round and round,
All day long.

... **wipers** ... go **swish, swish, swish!** ...
... **horn** ... goes **beep, beep, beep!** ...
... **driver** ... says **"Tickets, please!"** ...
... **money** ... goes **chink, chink, chink!** ...
... **bell** ... goes **ding, ding, ding!** ...
... **babies** ... go **wah, wah, wah!** ...
... **people** ... go **chitter, chatter, chatter!** ...

44

This old man

This old man, he played **one**.
He played knick knack on my **thumb**;
With a knick knack, paddy whack
Give a dog a bone,
This old man came rolling home.

... two ...	... shoe ...
... three ...	... tree ...
... four ...	... door ...
... five ...	... hive ...
... six ...	... sticks ...
... seven ...	... oven ...
... eight ...	... gate ...
... nine ...	... spine ...
... ten ...	... hen ...

Three blind mice

Three blind mice, three blind mice,
See how they run, see how they run.
They all ran after the farmer's wife
Who cut off their tales with a carving knife.
Did ever you see such a thing in your life
As three blind mice?

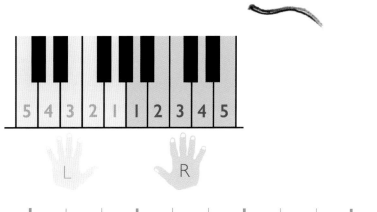

Twinkle, twinkle little star

Twinkle, twinkle, little star,
How I wonder what you are.
Up above the world so high,
Like a diamond in the sky.
Twinkle, twinkle, little star,
How I wonder what you are.

When the blazing sun is gone,
When he nothing shines upon,
Then you show your little light,
Twinkle, twinkle, all the night.
Twinkle, twinkle ...

In the dark blue sky you keep
And often through my curtains peep,
For you never shut your eye,
Till the sun is in the sky.
Twinkle, twinkle ...

As your bright and tiny spark
Lights the traveller in the dark,
Though I know not what you are,
Twinkle, twinkle, little star!
Twinkle, twinkle ...

Yankee Doodle

Yankee Doodle went to town,
A-riding on a pony.
He stuck a feather in his hat,
And called it macaroni.

Yankee Doodle doodle do,
Yankee doodle dandy,
All the lasses are so smart
And sweet as sugar candy.

5	4	3	2	1	1	2	3	4	5

L   R

R	1 1	2 3	1 3 2	1 1	2 3	1
L			3			1

	1 1	2 3	4 3 2 1		1	1
3				1 3 2 1		

			1			
2 1	2 3	2 1		3 2	3 4 5	3

		1	1	2 1	1
2 1	2 3	2 1	2 3	1	

Acknowledgements

No Notes piano music aims to make beginners' first piano experiences inspiring, fun and practically useful. I have been wonderfully supported in this by my sister Judy whose playful images provide an irresistible attraction to each song and an amusing distraction when the business of making music becomes, momentarily, overwhelming! I am very grateful too for many helpful comments and suggestions made by my family, friends and colleagues, especially Lizzie Higginson, Ben Lloyd, Sarah Lloyd, Bernardita Muñoz Chereau and Kate Miller. I'm very fortunate to have been guided through a variety of practical and technical challenges by Russ Davidson, Oliver Marler, Nadia Sheltawy and Anne Michèle de Deus Silva. Lastly, I want to thank my piano students who have taught me so much about learning and teaching and whose needs and wants have inspired and motivated me.

For Robin Autumn and Lola Moon - always music to my ears!